UNIVERSAL
MUSIC
THE NEW NOTE

BY

MRS. L. DOW BALLIETT

Author of

**"How to Attain Success Through the Strength
of Vibration: A System of Numbers as
Taught by Pythagoras," "Body Beauti-
ful,' "Musical Vibration of the
Speaking Voice," "Philos-
ophy of Numbers," their
Tone and Colors."**

**"Beyond Sight," "Nature's Symphony," "Balliett
Philosophy of Number Vibration, in
Questions and Answers."**

Published by the Author

1101 PACIFIC AVENUE, ATLANTIC CITY, N. J.

1922.

L. N. FOWLER & CO.
NO. 7 IMPERIAL ARCADE, LUDGATE CIRCUS
LONDON, E. C.

IF YOU ARE A PIONEER IN MUSIC
THIS LITTLE BOOK IS FAITHFULLY
DEDICATED TO YOU BY
THE AUTHOR

CONTENTS

Universal Music

New Note

WHEN we ask, "What is Music," and "Of what is its source," vibration of numbers answers the question, proving that each individual thing found in the mineral, vegetable and animal kingdom is the source and foundation of music.

Every leaf of the forest has its note which is heard by the all-hearing ear and would also be heard by ours if we lived in conscious relation with the Divine. We would hear the grass grow and hear the voice of all created things. This is true if we lived in tune with the Infinite.

Somewhere in every harmonious and inharmonious sound the spirit within the object causing the sound has power to send out the notes of the souls' overtones. These sounds are caught and held in the sky or the akashic records oft called "The Book of God's Remembrance." Anyone who can ascend high enough to near this source with balanced body, soul and spirit can bring back the "Song of Heaven," and place it in printed pages for the use of those who have not as yet found the path of the upward road; until then, they must use what the Master minds bring to them, knowing they too can ascend if they will simply trust and obey nature, by tuning their bodies as they do an instrument, always remembering music belongs to

Nature's realm, as do their own bodies and everything that has form is but borrowed from Nature, and must be returned; sometime in life's journey they will return all borrowed goods.

This universal system of music is a new note toward Nature's freedom. The fundamentals found in this book are for you to use and develop according to your own consciousness as revealed in your law of life. Use any time and key, preferably your own note of birth. Their silent notes are deeply embedded in your system. If a life has a law which moves it as does the sun and moon by Nature's mathematical precision, it is found in the month, day and year of your birth with their digits and silent notes. They show the law of this span of life, in

which you are living. The digit of
your birthpath strikes its own note
in the realm of spoken nature, thus
making you a part of all things, with
all things in the seen and unseen
world.

You are a trinity of body, soul and
spirit, so every note has three parts,
and when you voice any note there is
a majority of effect upon the silent
side of soul and spirit, and you must
be in harmony with your silent side
or your music is not music, but sounds.
Nature is ruled by the law of action
and compensation,—and to win you
must study the intellectual parts of
music. When the body is trained as
an instrument is tuned, ever hold on
to the intellect, but realize you are one
with Nature and the silent notes will

find expression through your body. To succeed in all musical rendition of another's work, one must unite their soul with the soul of the composer. The link lies in the silent notes, by loving the sounds of these notes and feeling that the instrument is but an extension of yourself, and you are but an open reservoir of melodious forces that Nature has loaned for your use,— then by placing your fingers on the keys of an instrument with blessings and love, sensitive ears, hear tones floating all about you—these are the silent notes of the dominant one you will strike, but the sweetest tones are those you feel through the harmony of your body, soul and spirit with that of the composer. When man passes beyond the realm of time, where suns do not rise or set, he carries in his soul the music he has absorbed during earth life. This he carries with him to other planes of existence, and it cannot be lost. No gift of God is ever lost. His soul and spirit are the silent notes he used while here. By faithful love and service, his body may become harmonious atoms and the audible earth note, though faltering, may join its sound with the two silent ones, thus the trinity of three becomes the one perfect sound. In this and in other realms much depends upon the fidelity, love and truth of the individual. We know nature always longs to express to man, whom she regards as God, her longings. She tries to tell him in the sounds of the earth, wind, water and fire, her stories of aspiration, but he stands mute before the gift God gave him dominion over,— that of nature,—his unknown child.

The trinity is present in everything found in the seen and unseen world. The Bible calls it "Father, Son and Holy Spirit,"—body, soul and spirit, —father, mother and child; in science, opaque, opalescent and transparent; in nature, unity, diversity and harmony. So everything has three parts. They may be a harmony or inharmony, but they will express the thing in its present state of development where it now is, during its upward climb toward a state of greater harmony and development. In its journey different forms of names will show out different vibrations, which show the present state of consciousness that it is functioning under. Man sees and judges every other man, and all things else by that state of consciousness he is functioning in. When he arises he lifts all things in the known world with him. His goal should be to reach the sky records where is stored pure music with all things else the heart desires. Man has used nature as his slave filling her air with curses and falsehood. And yet she has supplied him with materials with which, through his God given power, he has made instruments in accord with nature's law, and gladly she fills them for utility, melody or harmony, as near to perfection as they approach nature's perfect law. When man becomes what man should be, his body becomes all kinds of musical instruments. To assist this,

he must use his efforts to bring out
and understand every sound and
color, found in the letters of a word
as in the letters are found the consciousness of the thing, and the musical
notes express these sounds. Its crud-
ity at first may shock the ear, but by
using these notes in his own way his
effort will grow until he realizes what
Pythagoras meant by the "Music of
the Spheres."

I am preparing in a crude way
nature's language of music from
Pythagoras' law of letter vibration.
Associated with it is a Balliett musical chart, which is scientifically correct. If anything is true in the realm
of number vibration, then the note
comprising the letters of a thing is
their conscious relation of the thing

to the world and spirit—the same as a name given at birth shows the consciousness of the individual coming to this world—so in the notes of the name of everything are found the voice of all things in nature. They reach their height in the value of their letters or notes in the digit of the whole, and their spirit aspiration is found in the vowels of everything. These vowel sounds should be played upon the high keys of an instrument or used in any way with the voice. They are the whisperings of the soul. Only use the notes as they are found in the word, and emphasize the digit as the supreme height of the whole because they are the stronger part. Anything to be of practical use must be built upon the scientific basis of three, regardless of what name the three parts are called. A good definition of soul is given by the philosopher Delsarte who says "The soul is the highest plane of body, and the lowest of spirit." The soul is the plane of adjustment where nature finds the quiet spot which is present in all things where the forces gather and emerge. Sounds are adjusted therein, and emerge through the body out into the world of sound. The spirit is the foundation, the soul the adjuster, the audible sound the development of them both. In the human body or instrument they speak through the smile, the caress, the loves,—unspoken sounds they are, the part the musician must make his own until every note is felt and lives in his system, as the musician is but an instrument that must reflect nature. Until then he bears the relation to music as that of a worker. When the soul and spirit of every note is felt as a loved messenger, then one is ready to give forth their sounds to a world that is eagerly waiting for true, heart-felt music. In the execution, stop and listen to the inner voice of the spirit, how to touch the keys or sing the notes. It may differ from your former training in music, but you are now playing with the Universe and its new note. Nature is ruled with mathematical precision, so somewhere in every form there must be an underlying plan, a picture or ideal to be reached. Do this through your own law of life found by the digit of your birth number.

Be careful not to allow so-called guides to enter your body and dictate to you their wishes. Nature by inspiration reveals, but never controls, even though brilliant moments may temporarilly result with guidance, it never fails to destroy. To know the difference between Nature's God and obscession? One shows you the way, obscession takes control and you are not aware of the notes you strike or the selections you play or sing, you are using another's soul, your own is driven out. There are souls strongly developed in music who find pleasure in recalling unknown music upon instruments or in voice. So long as they are fully conscious of their surroundings and the music they are playing, Nature's friendly forces are their teacher and they are not obsessed.

Use the notes in foreign language as you make them from Charts No. 1 and 2. Use them in the same manner as is present in the English, the spirit of Universal Nature speaks in language so its own people can understand. In this way we hear the heart throbs of different races and creeds in the wail or joy of their music. Every word in every language expresses to them the true consciousness of the thing and how it longs to sound out its true voice from its still center, out into the cosmos of living things, where in the process of time all sounds meet and blend.

CHART No. 1

1 2 3 4 5 6 7 8 9

a b c d e f g h i

j k l m n o p q r

s t u v w x y z

The first chart which is found in Encyclopedias has descended from Pathagoras in the 6th Century before Christ, says every letter of the alphabet has its own notes of vibration and color. From it is found the numerical value of all names. Read each part of the name separately; find its value according to the letters in the name. Then find the sum of figures comprising each name and the digit. Read each period in regular order according to the vibration in each name. The digit of the whole name is the most important as it shows the quality and the supreme height the person was born with. The parts of the name now used show how the world regards him at the present time.

The digit of the birth path show what part in the great chorus of life they come to take. It cannot be changed. It must be met. It can be made harmonious or its opposite.

This Chart is reproduced from the Balliett Books on "Number Vibration."

CHART No. 2

c d e f g a b

1 2 3 4 5 6 7

8 9

22 expresses the octave D-D

11 expresses the octave C-C

Before this Chart was copyrighted by Mrs. L. Dow Balliett in "Success through Vibration" in 1905, there had been a confusion in Number vibration. As the trinity made by the Silent and Dominant notes had not been recognized, this chart places the Silent Notes on the two preceding notes before the audible one is struck which makes the three. This makes the sound of one and two become audible in the three, thus making the C the foundation note of music. Pathagoras divided the alphabet into nine parts. Our musical gamet has seven notes, a b c d e f g, so the master numbers of 8, 9, 22 and 11 also show master individuals, and these numbers or notes that show them can be used in freedom on a higher plane than the earth music of the seven notes. These notes hold all the earth sounds where music is audible. The notes above the gamet of earth sounds will be played anywhere, anyhow. They are untrammelled, uncontrolled, as in the name of any person or thing that vibrates the full ovtave of D-D or C-C. Remember anything that bears the digit of 8, 9, 22 or 11 should be master productions. If a composer has not reached their height from a fidelity to truth, he will use his own vibrations and will make good music, but they usually employ too largely the intellect, when the heart is Nature's function of music and is the instrument of circulation in that realm. A composer's music will satisfy those who have not reached his height of vibration.

CHART No. 3

Musical
Notes

Silent notes a-b made audible in c
"   "   b-c   "   "   "   d
"   "   c-d   "   "   "   e
"   "   d-e   "   "   "   f
"   "   e-f   "   "   "   g
"   "   f-g   "   "   "   a
"   "   g-a   "   "   "   b
"   " above a-b "   "   "   C
"   "   b-c "   "   "   D
"   "   B-C "   "   "   Octave of D-D
"   "   A-B "   "   "   Octave of C-C

In making original music or finding the vibration of anything use this chart in conjunction with Charts 1 and 2. This Chart should be studied until the notes are entirely memorized.

CHART No. 4

```
            11
        1   22   9
     2             8
        3        7
          4  6
            5
```

Shows the numerical value of numbers

In ancient days the moral foundation was founded upon "Be unto others as you would have others be unto you." As the fulfillment required dealing entirely with ones self, it was rewritten to comply with an easier code. "Do unto others as you would have them do unto you." The first required a high growth upon all planes and spoke through silent being, showing out as character. The latter is a removal of base into the world of action, which is governed by nature's law. We find it easier to "Do" than to "Be." So in music it is easier to do than to be. To *be* you will silently learn the correct tone of the notes, and as you breathe from a continuous force from earth to sky and from sky to earth within strike the two silent notes flowing into the audible sound. In doing this you find comradeship with being as you breathe from within to the without, and from the without to the within, from these notes play or sing the audible note. Give it a freedom of placement in your body, it may not be the old place, but let it show you its way. Mother Nature is a wise teacher, only remember the brain power must never sleep too long. After the cells in your body have assimilated them, no matter how fast the succession of sounds come there is a rapid response from your body to every note. Music then rests and invigorates instead of depleting. Your instrument becomes one with the cosmos and yourself, and everything living feels the contact of the sympathetic touch which you have consciously sought and gained for them.

In a soul's way of development, it takes many paths and devious ways to reach the ideal that was launched out into the cosmos somewhere along life's journey, and Mother Nature ever watchful tries to bring into expression the true wish of the soul she has clothed with a body. No name or time of birth can be an accident if we believe in the unwavering laws of nature. Every soul born in the flesh must bear as independent a life as does the sun and moon. The born ideal of your life is the goal through which your being moves. When you do not obey the captain of life's journey, you drift and suffer all kinds of ills which cloud your ideals and life becomes a shipwreck. But in silent moments you know within you a song of life is singing, telling you there is no outward circumstance that can keep you from the goal that your Soul's ideal set for you, only leaving it and going into the lives of others and blaming them can keep you from showing out the being there is within. Simply do your best and let others live their own lives. No doubt this present life is governed very much by your living of past ages. If you have gained power, when the cycle of so-called greatness empties you are great no matter where you are or what you are doing. All goodness and greatness is paid for in full by the ruler of the Heavens through earth. But no one can play well on an untuned instrument. You must do your part, or when the cycle opens and offers you the greatness of life, if you are untrue to man and God, you do not recognize the Master's gift; it passes on to return when you are more worthy. This is the law. When you do your very best in the place that you are living in and let others live their own lives, you will be moved higher to where you belong.

But you must deal entirely with the growth of your own self, knowing every trace of envy blocks the flow of nature's harmony. Only purity of life and in thought can a musician establish permanent success. Circumstances did not place you where you now are. Your higher self has put around you the material to work with, that is your soul's ideal. You may dislike your environment and all things pertaining to it, but it holds just the thing for triumph in overcoming self, to bring music out of discord.

ORIGINAL MUSIC

The making of original, individual music has been a great joy to many musicians. It has also been an incentive in the development of eurythmics; words with ideals of life should be set to the music of names and birth vibration. We will not use the musical staff, nor its key, but give the notes. You place them where you think they belong, using the initial notes as those of freedom and importance. They register above the world's gamet of seven note music. Their presence show that a master is present. You can use your own method of delineating your name, remember names show the consciousness of all things. No one should try to take a name they have not earned. The world feels the fraud and will not permanently accept a name that does not express the character of the person. A man or woman should use a name earned by degrees or marriage. No one can remain married, either of wife or husband, that have not earned the value of their vibrations. Use any part or combination of your name or mother's maiden name can be used. (Offices held, President vibrates eleven and sounds the whole octave of C-C.) Find the vowels of each name. They show the aspiration of the soul of the thing. Sometimes we live in them for hours or days, others seldom reach their height. Express them

upon the high keys with their silent
notes. These can be used as overtones or whispers becoming audible
in the dominant notes. Liberties can
be taken with names. They are ad-
justable and express our growth or
freedom. But the birthpath which
is our helper to growth cannot be
changed, it belongs to Nature's plane
and must be used as it appears, in
month, day and year. It must be
played as it is, as it was your choice
when you saw with the eye of spirit,
and nature recognizes no one who
tampers with her laws.

In making music use the birth
notes first, as a motif, and between
each name finishing also with the
same. Sometimes we wonder why we
chose such an inharmonious vibration

in which to express ourselves through life, but it now seems our part to bring as much harmony out of it as fidelity can show by its elevation. We cannot change it so try to elevate it in your own way. And you will bless the very air you live in. Finish all names with their digits, also their vowels; or spirit urge. Music must be finished by the combined digits of all names. Their vowels and the supreme heights of all the combined names.

We will use the name Eduard Hdgerup Grieg. Born June 15, 1843.

	Eduard		Colors	Silent Notes	Audible	Vowels		
E	vibrates	5	Pink	e f	g	e	f	g
d	"	4	Blue and Green	d e	f			
u	"	3	Yellow-flame	c d	e	c	d	e
a	"	1	Flame	a b	c	f	g	a
r	"	9	Red-Brown	b c	D	b	c	D
d	"	4	Blue-Green	bc fg	d a			
		26						
Plane of Adjustment		2		a b	c			
Add to find Digit		6						
		8						

Eight is the digit of Eduard and is a free number and note, Silent notes A-B, Audible C. Color of 8 or the free C note is Canary, found as the name is found.

			Silent notes c d	Audible e	Vowels or Spirit Urge with Silent Notes
CANARY					
c	vibrates	3	" " a b	"	c Silent a b Audible c
a	"	1	" " e f	"	g
n	"	5	" " a b	"	c " a b " c
a	"	1	" " B C	"	D
r	"	9	" " g a	"	b Digit of the whole
y	"	7	" " bc fg	"	DA vowels b C Audible D
Plane of Adjustment	26				
	2				
	6				
	8		" " a b	"	c

The color of 8 is canary. It is the free note of C, its silent notes a b. It also holds the colors of opal, which vibrates 8.

The name of Eduard shows the owner expressed in one third part of his system of body, soul and spirit a freedom in having passed beyond the earth limit of seven notes into the 8 of a Master body. (When any notes beyond a 7 or B note appear, it shows as one of freedom played or sung, in any way, or on any instrument with sharps or flats and is shown by the capital letters.) Numbers from one to seven are shown by small letters, excepting when the digit of the name is a free number (beyond 7 or the seven letters of the Scale). These letters are more intellectual but less expansive than the ones that have passed over the rim of the earth into cosmic freedom. These show the development of a master.

Hdgerup		Color	Silent Notes		Vowels
H vibrates	8	Canary, opal color	A B	Aud. Note C	
d "	4	Blue-Green	d e	" " f	
g "	7	Purple, steel brick	g a	" " b	
e "	5	Pink	e f	" " g	e f g
r "	9	Red, Brown	B C	" " D	
u "	3	Gold, flame	c d	" " e	c d e
p "	7	Purple, steel brick	g a	" " b	
Plane of	——		de cd	" " f e	
Adjustm't	43	Blue, green, gold			——
	4				A B C
	3				
	——				
	7				

Keynote of Hyderup is 7 the b note. This shows the height of the Jewish vibration. It is philosophically and intellectually mystical and refined with a finished elegance in music. It satisfies those who look alone for music as found in conventional codes. It is the earth vibration of 7, it shows

many m o u n t a i n s, it sometimes
ascends, and oftener descends into
the valleys where it r e j o i c e s in
nature's music. The colors this part
of his nature radiates are the sombre
colors of purple, steel and brick. It is
a proud number of lineage and desires
to return to the one rather than go on
to the eighth note. The spiritual urge
being a free C of eight, it urges him to
go on rather than return. This makes
him more active and more imagina-
tive than if his vowels were not free.
He also feels the presence of nature's
unseen children about him.

GRIEG		Colors	Silent Notes	Audible	Vowels
G	vibrtaes 7	Purple, steel brick	g a	b	
r	" 9	Red Brown	b c	D	b C audible D
i	" 9	" "	b c	D	e
e	" 5	Pink	e f	g	c d " e
g	" 7	Purple. steel brick	g a	b	e f
Plane of	—	Gold, flame, purple	cd ga	e b	g
Adjustment	37	steel brick			

$$\begin{array}{r} 3 \\ 7 \\ \hline 10 \end{array} \qquad \begin{array}{r} 1 \\ 0 \\ \hline 1 \end{array}$$

The supreme height is reached in one, color, Gold, flame. Silent notes a b audible c.

The keynote of Grieg is one or 1 0. It lacks one point of making the much desired eleven, which expresses the whole octave of C-C. This throws his active consciousness into Nature's music rather than into the scholarly classics of 8, 9, 22 and 11. The C note is both limited and unlimited. When with master minds unlimited, with earth notes finds itself representing nature's music of all things. It radiates a flame of many kinds of fuel.

Eduard vibrates	8	Silent Notes	a b	Audible	C
Hdgerup "	7	"	" ga	"	b
Grieg "	1	"	" a b	"	c
	—				
Plane of Adj.	16				
	1	"	" ab fg	"	c a
	6				
	—				
	7	"	" ga	"	b

	Vowels			
Eduard	Silent Notes	e f	audible	g
	" "	c d	"	e
	" "	f g	"	a
	" "	B C	"	D
Hdgerup	" "	e f	"	g
	" "	A B	"	C
Grieg	" "	B C	"	D
	" "	e f	"	g
The whole vowels		B C	"	Octave of D D

The keynote of this composer is seven, expressed by the b note with g a silent. As all seven music is philosophical but in a manner lacks freedom of unlimited flights essential to satisfactory music. So would we find Grieg's music, but within his system his vowels value 22, a full octave of D-D, showing he has an active spiritual mind co-operating with his physical being. When living on the heights, he is able to see through earth's dust, and there strikes all the notes of octave D-D. At other times when within the limit of 7 his music is the song of earth i n s t e a d of Heaven; a name expressing 22 is more abiding than the urge of the spirit found in vowels. He chose to be born June 15, 1843.

		Silent Note
June vibrates 6 colors, scarlet, orange, heliotrope		fg audible a
Day digit " 6 " " " "		fg " a
Year digit " 7 " " steel, purple, brick		ga " b
Plane of —		
Adjustment 19 " Flame, red brown		ab bc " CD

1
9
—
10
—1
0
—1

1 Color Flame, Silent Notes of birthpath ab audible C

His birthplace is one or C. This is an ambitious vibration as the vowels of one are of value eleven, showing a desire to sound the full octave of C-C instead of one or C note. The digits of month and day show him to be a cosmic mother whose vibration is 6 and strikes the A note. His year or silent master is the earth forces. His success lies in alert listening to all things that come to him and expressing them in his own way. His body is atuned to the C note, his soul and spirit act through a b c, he hears music through these notes. He should use them as keynotes to his writings and expression. His spirit is urging him to use the octave of D as shown by the desire of his vowels. In this, wisdom would show in accepting the help offered. The colors found by the digit of his month, day and year are interwoven into the fiber of his being. They tinge everything he sees, and touches through this pause in life's journey.

The C note is a vibration of flame, its color shows out according to the fuel used. It must help all others or suffer a crucifixion. Kama was made a god because he was a friend to every living thing.

Musicians are inclined to sign their music using different parts of their name, usually the vibration shows the quality of its production if it is below in vibration to the sublime height of the composer's consciousness, we find less struggle than when he goes beyond his own limit. The music of a composer is usually satisfactory to those who have not reached the height of consciousness of the composer.

The strongest part of Eduard Hagerup Grieg's system is found in his vowel or spirit side of his nature which shows in a more masterly manner than his objective life. The whispered vowel notes of Eduard are silent e f and audible g, and silent a b and audible c. Adjustment Silent notes B C audible D; of Hdgerup, silent notes e f audible g, silent notes a b audible, digit silent notes A B audible C; vowels of Grieg, silent notes B C audible D, silent notes e f audible G, value silent notes e f audible g; value of all the vowels, silent B C and D, silent notes A. B. audible C — Silent notes e f audible g—Silent A B audible C—Silent notes g a audible b — Silent e f and audible g. The vowels of whole name, octave of D-D.

To summarize the meaning of notes and numbers we spell all names used as we do the names of individuals; there is no guess work in colors or notes or their character.

C or one note means creation, unity. Is an adept. Color flame.

D or 2 notes means collecting. Is a seer. Color gold.

E or 3 " " expressing c and d. Is an adept and seer. Color gold and flame.

F or 4 " " physical and mental force. Its color blue and green.

G or 5 " " new life. A sage. Color pink.

A or 6 " " a cosmic Mother, Priest. Colors scarlet, orange, heliotrope.

B or 7 " " earth, its joys and shadows. Colors purple, steel.

C or 8 " " above the earth's gamut. Rejuvenation. A mystic. Canary, opal.

D or 9 " " above the earth's gamut. Law and full expression on all planes. Color red and brown.

Octave 22 of D-D means a master co-operative. Color cream.

Octave 11 of C-C means exaltation, a master mystic. Colors violet, yellow, black and white.

The musical notes of birth and name of Eduard Hdgerup Grieg.

To set name and birth to Music.

Motif of birth or birth numbers.

Birth motif Silent notes f g audible

notes A; silent notes f g, audible note A; silent notes f g audible note A. Silent notes g a audible note b. Mystical soul plane of adjustment; silent notes a b, audible C; silent notes B C, audible note D; audible C D. These notes resolve themselves in the digit of his birthpath and express him as the vibration of C. Silent notes A b, audible C, follow this with first name Eduard. Silent notes e f, audible g, silent notes d e, audible f, silent notes c d, audible e, silent notes a b, audible C, silent notes B C, audible D, silent notes d e, audible f. Plane of adjustment mystical. Silent notes B C, audible D, silent notes F G, audible A, Digit of the whole. Silent notes A B audible C. Put in here the vowels.

Put in here the motif of birth digit.

Silent notes f g, audible a, silent notes f g, audible a, silent notes g a, audible b, soul plane which is mystical a b, audible C, silent notes B C, audible C D. play with the strength of the whole. The note he chose for his guardian spirit, silent notes a b, audible note C.

Put in here next name, Hdgerup. Silent notes A B, audible C, silent notes d e, audible f, silent g a, audible b; silent e f, audible g; silent note B C, audible D, silent notes c d, audible E, silent notes g a, audible b, mystical plane of adjustment. Silent notes d e, audible f, silent notes c d, audible e, the strength of the whole in digit of name. Silent g a, audible b, vowels which are whispered. Silent notes e f, audible g, silent c d, audible e, silent a b, audible c.

Put in here next name, Grieg. Grieg —silent notes g a, audible b, silent notes B C, audible D, silent notes B. C, audible D, silent notes e f, audible g, silent notes g a, audible b, plane of adjustment. Mystical. Silent, c d, audible e, silent notes g a, audible b, strongest of the whole, a b, dominant C. Vowels whispered on high keys, silent notes B C, audible D, silent notes e f, audible g, silent notes e f, audible g.

Put in here Birth-path.

Put in here all his names and their digits with spirit urge and silent notes.

Eduard—silent notes A B, audible

C, spiritual urge play on high keys, silent e f, audible g, silent notes f g, audible a, silent notes for the whole a b, audible C.

Put in here Birth motif.

Hdgerup—silent notes g a, audible b, spiritual urge e f, audible g, silent notes a b, audible b for the whole name of silent notes g a, audible b, silent notes A B, audible C.

Put in here Birth motif.

Grieg—silent notes, a b, audible C, spirit urge B C, audible D, silent notes e f, audible g.

Put in here Birth motif.

Whole name, silent notes A. B. audible C, silent notes g a, audible b, silent notes a b, audible C, his entire key-

note; silent notes g a, audible b, his
entire spiritual urge; e f, audible g,
silent notes f g, audible a, silent notes
B C, audible D, silent notes e f, audible g, spirit urge of whole being E F,
audible G, silent notes A B, audible
note C, silent notes b c, audible D, silent notes e f, audible g, whole of spiritual urge octave D-D.

End with Birth motif.

TIME, HARMONY, MELODY

When we examine through vibration of numbers the active principles of music, Time, Harmony and Melody, we see three parts as living beings each taking their place in the great symphony of sounds.

Time stands between creation and expression, it is Creation, it is a Time Keeper, a helper to expression.

Notes found by Charts 1 and 2 show time's conscious relation to all things. The notes portray Time found by Chart 1.

Consciousness of Time

Time	Plane of Adjustment	Vowels
2 9 4 5	20 - 2	i e
		- 14 Digit 5

Found by Chart 3

Silent notes b c, audible d, silent notes B C, audible D, silent notes d e, audible f, silent notes e f, audible g, plane of adjusting nature into spirit. Silent notes b c, audible d, silent notes of digit b c, audible d. Vowels played on high keys in whispered tones. Silent notes B C, audible D, silent notes e f, audible g, plane of adjustment, silent notes a b, audible c, silent notes d e, audible f, Digit. Silent notes e f, audible g. Time is the physical basis for spiritual structure. It belongs to nature's realm. When we pass beyond nature's realm there is nothing to count time with.

CONSCIOUSNESS OF HARMONY

Harmony	Plane of Adjustment	Vowels
8 1 9 4 6 5 7	40	a o
		1 6 - 7

The keynote of Harmony is four. It means a unity of the cosmos with earth.

Its Notes Found by Chart 3

Silent notes A B, audible C, silent notes a b, audible c, silent notes B C audible D, silent notes d e, audible f, silent notes f g, audible a, silent notes e f, audible g, silent notes g a, audible b. Adjustment silent notes d e, audible f, vowels silent notes a b, audible

c, silent notes f g, audible a, Digit.
Silent notes g a, audible b.

Found by Chart 3

CONSCIOUSNESS OF MELODY

Melody	Plane of Adjustment	Vowels
4 5 3 6 4 7	29 - 11	e o
		5 6-value 11

Silent notes d e, audible f, silent
notes e f, audible g, silent notes c d,
audible e, silent notes f g, audible a,
silent notes d c, audible f, silent notes
g a, audible b, silent notes B C, audible
D, Spirit Octave of C-C. Vowels.
Silent notes e f, audible g, silent notes
f g, audible a. Keynotes of melody
of vowels. The whole octave of C-C.

The notes in Melody reach the most
exalted height of spirit. They can be

played upon any part of the instrument or voice. The vowels also show they are in harmony with the physical structure or letters both showing the highest of all vibration, the eleven or octave of C-C.

SONG OF LIFE

Everything has its own song—it sings all through the day and through the night. The cosmos sings its own song. We hear it according to the different position of the earth to our human ears, but the song goes on and on and in its heart is the notes of your and my life tuned to the cosmic sounds of the month, day and year of our birth, as they are seldom the same, so we each day approach our song from a different viewpoint of time, harmony or melody. Sometimes the notes clash as every day has its own note, also its own color. So one song is sometimes silenced by the discord present in our own bodies and in the cosmos. The day Eduard Hdgerup Grieg was born, June 15, 1843.

The digit of June is month	6	silent notes	f g	audible	a
" " " Day was	6	" "	f g	"	a
" " " Year is	7	" "	ga	"	b

$$\begin{array}{r} 19 \\ \hline 1 \\ 9 \\ \hline 1 \end{array}$$

Digit of combined vibration of birth is 1.

This throws him into Nature's trinity of one, two, three. The day he was born, the first sound his infant ears heard was the fundamental C which rang out as the dominant note of the day. Silent notes a b, dominant C. Every cell in his body was attuned to these notes and ever afterwards he heard music through these sounds. The C note was the spirit of his present life, he heard the earth notes of the month as silent f g, audible a. He heard the same sounds in days and the slow revolving year as the teacher or, master in the silent notes g a audible b, and the f u n d a m e n t a l silent notes of a, b, audible C. These notes form the basis of his song of life. He could do his best work in the C sound and the notes of his month, day and year always held him to their charm. As they with their vibrating colors showed him his law of life, as he was built of the one vibration, so we naturally know his life is touched by anything whose digit is one as 10, 19, 28, 37, 46, and all the way through all combinations that show their digit of spirit as one. They touch the well-spring of nature's rule in his life.

His life song sings as silent notes f g, audible a, silent notes f g, audible a, silent notes g a, audible b, plane of musical adjustment, silent notes a b, audible C, silent notes B C, audible D, spirit silent notes a b, audible C. If you wish to go further, the vowels of one are of value 11, these vibrate to octave of C-C. This is repeated. The vowels of b or seven are again one in the two fives of seven. This makes another octave of C-C. This height is found in Octave C-C. (Repeat). Silent notes ga, audible B. Every musician should know his success in musical composition is greatly advanced by using his own keynote, as the key to his music. We understand music through our own keynote as it is the point of contact between others, notes and our own hearing, we judge Music through its quality. Grieg's as a one or C, birthpath touched all sounds as C is the string which holds all other notes together.

COLOR

Through a lack of scientific adhesion and understanding, there has been a confusion in the color of different notes. In this free study of music we must open ourselves to every train of reasoning as only in this way can we find what is a truth to the world and to ourselves, and thus hold fast to any power that aids in our development. We know things seen are elusive on this earth plane where we see color. So in it we must look for a scientific basis and hold to it firmly in all its parts until we find its reality of truth. Every person is as much a planet as is the one he walks

upon which is governed by its own
laws and is in a state obedient to a
higher national law. So must our
system governed by ourselves be in
harmony and obedient to God's law in
nature. As all the planets in the star-
ry heavens have their own notes and
color (which is found by the name
they bear), so our planet named
"body" has its own color and note
and is found by adding the letters of
the name we bear, which is not an ac-
cidental thing, nor is the month, day
and year we chose to be born in an accident. Through this law we see our
own law of life. Through the digit of
birth number we also see the period of
recurring events, and with its silent
notes we see the spiritual process be-
hind the world's events. We each see

through the color of month, day and year of our own birth according to the government of our own body. We see some note show out blue when another born in the yellow light sees it as the color that tinges all things throughout his life. He is tuned to his own colors and sounds and through his own note to those things whose language we do not understand. They know him by his vibrating note and color. He sees through his own viewpoint, through his own color and sound and plane where such sights and sounds are audible. There must be a universal rule in regard to color as to sounds; a scientific basis, through which color must take its place. Each note has its color, thus the major part of every sound is upon

the silent side of life. The side where
everything is born from a steam en-
gine to all works of art, the colors lie
hidden in every note like the radiance
in a diamond or opal. So the audible
note holds within its system the two
other parts and their color which may
be of a different character from the
audible sound. The philsopher Delsarte says when the body shows great
physical strength the spirit is in a
state of weakness, and when spirit is
strong, the body shows less vigor, so
we find notes to be used for
such purposes to portray a subject,
such notes with the character neces-
sary as express the g notes in one of
the most subjective and mystical of all
notes. It is made from the combination of e f and audible in g, it seems to

be taken with bated breath from without, while the A note made from f g, sounds out an independent sound from within to the without.

To prove these colors are scientifically correct, spell them out from Chart 1 as you do your name, thus proving by The Balliett system of analysis of words, they must be spelled out to find a scientific basis for colors and all things else. If one part is true, then all things are true, and the colors given here are true or there is no truth in vibrating numbers. Find many other colors by vibrating their name by Chart 1.

The silent colors of a and b are scarlet, orange and heliotrope with purple, steel and brick. Their audible color shows out as C in yellow, flame.

The silent colors of b and c are purple, steel brick and yellow, flame of gold. Their audible colors show by note d and is a blue and green color.

The silent color of C and d are gold, blue and green and show out as E a yellow, flame.

Silent colors of d and e, blue and green, gold, gold flame, and yellow. They show out as f, blue and green.

Silent colors of e and f are yellow, flame, blue and green, show out as g, pink.

Silent colors of f g blue, green, pink, show out as a, color orange, scarlet and heliotrope.

Silent colors of g a, are pink, orange, scarlet, heliotrope, show out in b. purple, steel, brick.

Silent colors of the eight notes above the world's gamet of sound are scarlet, orange, heliotrope, purple, steel, brick, show out canary, and opal colors.

Silent colors of D above the world's music are purple, steel, brick, canary, opal colors, show out in a, gold, flame, red and brown.

Silent colors of Octave of D-D are canary, opal and purple, steel brick. Show out all shades of gold, red and cream.

Silent colors of octave C-C are all shades of purple, canary, opal colors and red, show out a yellow violet, black and white.

The silent notes a b, audible C. The a note shows more cosmic color than any other. It is a cosmic mother it

holds scarlet, heliotrope and orange,
also it shows the shadows always present in the b note which is an earth note
and expresses home ties and blood relations. Its color is purple, steel brick.
This combination in nature's laboratory shows out in the foundation notes
of C and shows from their colors a
flame and holds in dilution the fundamental colors of red, yellow and blue.

Silent notes of b and c show purple,
steel brick and flame, and becomes
audible in D, and shows out a blue and
green color. This is a bold, daring intellectual color- note and will fight and
defend as only a four character can
do.

Silent color of c and d are a yellow,
flame and with blue and green, which
shows Heaven and earth as a passing

flame. They show out as pink in g. As the vibration of the Christ is mystical and holds unknown depths.

Silent notes of f g holds colors of blue and green that must be harmonized to live together, when they show out as pink in the a note, which reflects from this strong combination of earth "The blue" and Christ's color of pink, into scarlet, orange and heliotrope.

Silent colors of g a are pink, scarlet, heliotrope and orange, yet from this radiant center the b note shows out with sombre colors of purple, steel brick. It seems like joy clothed in black.

The silent colors above the ordinary plane of music in a b show out more radiant colors of scarlet, heliotrope, orange, purple and steel than the plane of earth's music. It shows out as canary and opal colors, it means a master body.

Silent colors of b c above the ordinary gamut of sound and sight holds purple and flame and becomes audible in D all shades of red, blue and green.

22 expresses the octave of D-D and the reds and browns and gold are the dominating colors.

11 expresses the octave of C-C. The spiritual colors are yellow, black, white and violet. This last color is borrowed from the gamut of colors beyond our normal sight.

The A note is like a sky at sunset. One watches its beauty while strange emotions fill one as to what it is or means.

The b note is like joy clothed in black. It has a radiant center of glorious cosmic colors, but only when she unloosens her mantel will the joy of life come out into the world and show its strength.

The c note holds the joy of radiance of the cosmos with its shadows. It burns as a flame to lighten the paths of others.

D note holds the human shadows of humanity and by action lights a flame to build or destroy. The action must go on be it militant or idealistic according to its surroundings, it gathers and holds.

E has its torch lighted and feels every idealistic or militant emotion that presents itself, but it lets others carry their burdens while it enjoys their blessings, it expresses in every way of earth the struggle with the unseen.

F is a militant note. It is always ready for a fray. Yet no evil enters the yellow center of its heart.

G is the metaphysical note of pink. It means new life yet from the struggle of the silent note of e and f in its system, it gives out somewhat of a careless joy, a changeable nature from subconscious to conscious, without thought or argument. It is a very dawn of morning instead of sunset, fascinating and youthful. It seems to speak from the without to the within of unseen things with bated breath.

A is a cosmic note with a heart of storms and sunshine, A bearing of burdens yet not knowing how to drop them as the g note of pink from the center of its being suggests. It sustains and creates. It seems to speak from the within in a bold voice of nature.

B is a sad yet oftimes happy note, desiring to turn back and go over the old road of ancestry. It holds all of earth's vibrations and loves to express nature's views—it expresses the earth.

C is the foundation note of air and water—it holds in its center the feeling of equality.

C on plane above the normal gamut shows resurrection and a collection of things seen in the world of sounds and colors.

D is a human note and understands any other note if given a chance to comrade with it, it is a master of law.

The octave of D-D is a master of law and love upon all planes.

The octave of C-C is a master of psychic understanding upon all planes.

SOME OF THE SILENT VOICES

Consciousness of Water found by Chart 1.

W a t e r   Mystical adjustment
5 1 2 5 9 added   22
     Do not add 22 or 11. Water
     vibrates 22. Its vowels a e
     value 6.

Find Musical Notes by Chart 2

Play silent e f, audible g, silent a b, audible c, silent b c, audible d, silent e f, audible g, silent b c, audible d, Plane of Adjustment, mythical B C, audible D, silent note B. C audible D, Supreme height of water is found in whole octave of D-D. Its spirits urge of vowels silent a b, audible c, silent e f, audible g, silent or height of vowels, silent a b. audible c, silent e f, audible g, silent f g, audible a.

CONSCIOUSNESS OF FIRE

F i r e

6 9 9 5   added 29

$$
\begin{array}{r}
2 \\
9 \\
\hline
11
\end{array}
$$

Do not add the 11. It sands for all colors and the octave of C-C. Vowels i e, value 5.

Find musical notes of fire by Table 2

Play. Silent f g, audible, a, silent notes B C, audible D, silent notes B C, audible D, silent e f, audible g. It reaches its height in full octave of C-C.

Its spiritual urge found silent B C audible D, silent e f, audible g, its height silent e f, audible g.

Consciousness of Earth found by Chart 1.

E a r t h   Mystical adjustment

5 1 9 2 8   added 25   Add to find
                                        digit or height.

                              2

                              5

                              —

7 Seven is the digit of earth.

Notes of earth found by Chart 2 played, silent notes e f, audible g, silent a b, audible c, silent B C, audible D, silent b c, audible d, silent A B, audible C, Mystical adjustment bC, audible d, silent e f, audible g. Supreme height of earth. Silent g a, audible b. vowels whispered on high keys, silent e f, audible g. Silent a b, audible c, digit of vowels. Silent note f g, audible a. Express earth, silent notes g a, audible b. Earth is limited in vibration. A finished number.

CONSCIOUSNESS OF AIR

A i r   Mystical adjustment

1 9 9 — 19

$$\begin{array}{r} 1 \\ 9 \\ \hline 10 \end{array}$$ Add to find digit or height.

$$\begin{array}{r} 1 \\ 0 \\ \hline 1 \end{array}$$

One is the keynote of air and belongs to nature's trinity. It holds two master numbers of free D.

Play by musical key 2. Silent notes a b, audible C, silent notes b c, audible D, silent b C, audible D, Mystical adjustment a b, audible C, silent b C, audible D, height of whole, silent a b, audible C, Vowels whisper B C, audible D.

CONSCIOUSNESS OF WIND

W i n d   Plane of adjustment

5 9 5 4   added   23

                        2

                        3

                        —

                        5   Add to find digit

Find musical notes by Chart 2

Play, Silent notes e f, audible g, silent notes B. C, audible D, silent notes e f audible g, silent notes b c audible d, silent notes B C audible D. Mystical plane of adjustment silent e f audible g. Spirit wind whispered, silent b c audible d. To find many expressions of wind add East, West, North and South winds.

Find by Chart 1.

CONSCIOUSNESS OF NORTH

North	Plane of Adjustment	Digit	Vowels or Spirit Urge
5 6 9 2 8	Added 30	3	6

Find notes by musical chart No. 2

Silent notes, e f, audible g, silent notes f g, audible a, silent notes B C, audible D, silent notes b c, audible d, Silent notes A B, audible C, mystical plane of adjustment silent a b, audible c, spirit urge whispered silent f g, audible a.

Find by Chart 2.

CONSCIOUSNESS OF SOUTH

South	Plane of Adjustment	Digit	Vowels
1 6 3 2 8	Added 20	2	6

Play. Silent notes a b, audible C, silent notes f g, audible a, silent notes c d, audible e, silent notes b c audible d, silent notes A B, audible C. Mystical plane of adjustment, silent notes b C, audible note d, silent notes b c, audible d.

CONSCIOUSNESS OF EAST

East	Plane of Adjustment	Digit of East	Vowels or Spirit Urge
5 1 1 2	9	9	e a - 6

Silent notes e f, audible g, silent notes a b, audible c, silent notes a b, audible c, silent notes b c, audible d, Mystical like a question. Silent notes B C, audible D, Digit of East, silent notes B C, audible D. Vowels on high keys, silent notes e f, audible g, silent notes f g, audible a.

Digit of vowels silent notes f g, audible a.

CONSCIOUSNESS OF WATERFALL

Water	-	fall	Plane of Adjustment
5 1 2 5 9	22	6 1 3 3	- 13 - 22 and 4

Silent notes e f, audible g, silent a b, audible c, silent b c, audible d, silent e f, audible g, silent B C audible D. Adjustment Octave of D-D, Octave of D-D. Vowels silent notes a b, audible c, silent notes e f, audible g, digit of vowels, f g, audible a, Notes of Fall. Silent notes f g, audible a, silent notes a b, audible c, silent notes c d, audible e, silent notes c d, audible e, Plane of adjustment, silent notes a b, audible c, silent notes c d, audible e, Digit of fall, silent notes d e, audible f, Play together or separate.

CONSCIOUSNESS OF HAIL

H a i l	Plane of Adjustment	Digit of Hail	Vowels
8 1 9 3	21	3	a i
			6 5 - 11

Silent notes A B, audible C, silent notes a b, audible c, silent notes B C, audible D, silent notes c d, audible d. Plane of adjustment b c, audible d, silent notes a b, audible c, digit of hail, silent notes c d, audible e, vowels, silent f g, audible a, silent notes e f, audible g. The whole octave of C-C.

Consciousness of Sunshine

Sunshine	Plane of Adjustment	Digit of Sunshine	Vowels
1 3 5 1 8 9 5 5	37	1	u i e
			3 9 5-17-8

Silent notes a b, audible c, silent notes c d, audible e, silent notes e f, audible g, silent notes a b, audible c, silent notes A B, audible C, silent notes B C, audible D, Silent notes e f, audible g, repeat. Plane of adjustment c d, audible e, silent notes g a, audible b. Digit of whole vowels, silent notes c d, audible e, silent notes B C, audible D, silent notes e f, audible g, Plane of adjustment, silent notes a b, audible c, silent notes g a, audible b, Digit of whole A B, audible C. Vowels. Silent Notes A b, Audible C—

CONSCIOUSNESS OF WINTER

Winter	Plane of Adjustment	Digit	Vowels
5 9 5 2 5 9	35	8	i e
			9 5 - 15 - 5

Silent notes e f, audible g, silent notes B. C, audible D, silent notes e f, audible g, silent notes b c, audible d, e f audible g, silent notes B C audible D. Adjustment silent c d, audible e, silent notes e f, audible g. Digit A B, audible C. Vowels Silent B C and audible D, silent notes e f, audible g, Adjustment, silent notes a b, audible c, silent notes d e, audible f, Digit of whole of vowels, silent notes e f, audible g.

CONSCIOUSNESS OF SPRING

Spring	Plane of Adjustment	Digit	Vowels
1 7 9 9 5 7	38	11	9

Silent notes a b, audible c, silent notes g a, audible b, silent notes B. C audible D, Repeat. Silent notes e f, audible g, silent notes g a, audible b. Plane of Adjustment silent notes c d, audible e, silent notes A. B, audible C. Keynote Octave C-C. Vowels Silent b C, audible D.

CONSCIOUSNESS OF RIVULET

Rivulet	Plane of Adjustment	Digit	Vowels
9 9 4 3 3 5 2	35	8	9 3 5-17-8

Silent notes B C, audible D, Repeat. Silent notes d e, audible f, silent notes c d, audible e, Repeat. Silent notes e f, audible g, silent notes b c, audible d, Plane of adjustment, Silent notes c d, audible e, silent notes e f, audible g. Digit, silent notes A. B. Audible C.

CONSCIOUSNESS OF STORM

Storm	Plane of Adjustment	Vowels
1 2 6 9 4	22	6

Silent notes a b, audible c, silent notes b c, audible d, silent notes f g, audible a, silent notes B C, audible D, silent notes d e, audible f, Keynotes of the whole octave D-D, Vowels Silent f g and audible a.

CONSCIOUSNESS OF SUMMER

Summer	Plane of Adjustment	Vowels
1 3 4 4 5 9	26	3 5 - 8

Silent notes a b, audible c, silent notes c d, audible e, silent notes d e, audible f, Repeat. Silent notes e f, audible g, silent B C, audible D, Plane of Adjustment b c, audible d, silent f g, audible a. Digit, silent notes A B, audible C. Vowels silent notes c d, audible e, silent notes e f, audible g. Digit of vowels silent notes A B, audible C.

CONSCIOUSNESS OF AUTUMN

Autumn	Plane of Adjustment	Vowels
1 3 2 3 4 5	18 - 9	1 3 3 - 7

Silent notes a b, audible c, silent notes c d, audible e, silent notes b d, audible d, silent notes c d, audible e, silent notes d e, audible f, silent notes e f, audible g. Plane of Adjustment silent notes a b, audible c, silent notes A B, audible C. Digit of vowels, silent notes g a, audible b.

CONSCIOUSNESS OF CALM

Calm	Plane of Adjustment	Vowels
3 1 3 4	11	1

Silent notes c d, audible e, silent notes a b, audible c, silent notes c d, audible e, silent notes d e, audible f, Plane of Adjustment, silent notes A B, audible C, Repeat. Octave of C-C. Vowels silent notes a b, audible C.

CONSCIOUSNESS OF OCEAN

O c e a n	Plane of Adjustment	Digit	Vowels
6 3 5 1 5	20	2	6 5 1 - 12 -3

Silent notes f g, audible a, silent notes a b, audible c, silent notes e f, audible g, silent notes a b, audible c, silent notes e f, audible g, Adjustment, silent notes b c, audible d, silent notes b c, audible d. Vowels, silent notes f g, audible a, silent notes e f audible g, silent notes a b, audible c. Plane of adjustment silent notes b c, audible a, silent notes b c, audible d, Digit silent notes c d, audible e.

CONSCIOUSNESS OF SEA

S e a	Plane of Adjustment	Vowels
1 5 1	7	5

Silent notes a b audible c, silent notes e f, audible g, silent notes a b, audible c, digit, silent notes g a, audible b, vowels silent e f, audible g.

CONSCIOUSNESS OF LAKE

L a k e	Plane of Adjustment	Vowels
3 1 2 5	11	1 5 - 6

Silent notes c d, audible e, silent notes a b, audible c, silent b c, audible d, silent e f, audible g, Plane of Adjustment, silent notes a b, and audible

c, Repeat.   Octave of C-C.   Vowels
silent notes a b audible c, silent notes
e f audible g, digit of vowels, silent
notes f g, audible a.

CPSIA information can be obtained
at www.ICGtesting.com
Printed in the USA
LVHW061425160721
692898LV00012B/922

9 781162 596303